Encounters with God

The First Epistle of Paul the Apostle to the CORINTHIANS

Encounters with God Study Guide Series

The Gospel of Matthew

The Gospel of Mark

The Gospel of Luke

The Gospel of John

The Book of Acts

The Book of Romans

The First Epistle of Paul the Apostle to the Corinthians

The Second Epistle of Paul the Apostle to the Corinthians

The Epistle of Paul the Apostle to the Galatians

The Epistle of Paul the Apostle to the Ephesians

The Epistle of Paul the Apostle to the Philippians

The Epistles of Paul the Apostle to the Colossians and Philemon

The First and Second Epistles of Paul the Apostle to the Thessalonians

The First and Second Epistles of Paul the Apostle to Timothy and Titus

The Epistle of Paul the Apostle to the Hebrews

The Epistle of James

The First and Second Epistles of Peter

The First, Second, and Third Epistles of John and Jude

The Revelation of Jesus Christ

Encounters with God

The First Epistle of Paul the Apostle to the CORINTHIANS

CONTENTS

An Introduction to the Epistle of 1 Corinthians 7

An Overview of Our Study of the Epistle of 1 Corinthians 11

The Lessons:

LESSON #1: Spiritual Wisdom 15

LESSON #2: Sexual Purity. 25

LESSON #3: Self-Denial 37

LESSON #4: The Lord's Supper 47

LESSON #5: Spiritual Gifts 55

LESSON #6: Supremacy of Love. 67

LESSON #7: A Celestial Body. 77

Notes to Leaders of Small Groups. 85

AN INTRODUCTION TO THE EPISTLE OF 1 CORINTHIANS

The Book of 1st Corinthians is an "epistle"—a formal letter intended to give instruction. The letter was written by the apostle Paul to a vibrant, growing church in the highly cosmopolitan Greek city of Corinth. It addresses ethical, doctrinal, and practical problems that had arisen in the newly established church.

The church at Corinth was established by Paul about 50 AD during Paul's second missionary journey. In Corinth, Paul apparently stayed with a Jewish convert named Aquila and his wife Priscilla, and worked alongside them as a tentmaker even as he ministered the Gospel in the local synagogue. The Jews openly opposed his testimony that Jesus is the Christ (Messiah), so he began to preach and teach in the house of a man named Justus, next door to the synagogue. The account of Paul's ministry in Acts 18 tells us that "many of the Corinthians, hearing, believed and were baptized," including Crispus, the ruler of the synagogue (See Acts 18:8). In all, Paul was in Corinth about 18 months.

Corinth was the political capital of Greece and the seat of its commercial and intellectual life during the first century. Located on a narrow isthmus of land, it was at the crossroads of land travel from northern Greece and the Peloponnese, and the shipping routes between East and West. The city had a reputation for luxury and has been called by some historians the "emporium of Mediterranean trade." Because of its location and prosperity, Corinth attracted a massive influx of people from many cultures, races, and religions—businessmen, philosophers, tradesmen, and artists from all parts of the known world. The city had a very large slave population. Some historians estimate that in Paul's day the city had about 400,000 slaves and 250,000 free people. The church in Corinth reflected the cultural and socio-economic diversity of the city, including Jews, Romans, Greeks, aristocrats, and slaves.

Centuries before Paul, Corinth was the site of the temple of Aphrodite, the goddess of love, where hundreds of temple prostitutes had plied their trade. Corinth had been destroyed totally in 146 BC, but the Greeks quickly reinstituted goddess worship when the city was rebuilt by the Romans a hundred years later. Roman deities, as well as eastern mystery cults of Asia and Egypt, were introduced to Corinth. At least 26 temples and sacred places were built to honor rituals designated to a wide variety of beliefs. More than a thousand male and female prostitutes continued to service the worship of Aphrodite. It is little wonder that in Paul's time, the city had a reputation for both sexual vice and so-called "sacred" prostitution. In fact, the Greek language adopted a term "corinthianize," which meant "to practice sexual immorality."

It was while Paul was in Ephesus on his third missionary journey—documented in Acts 19—that he received disturbing reports of sexual immorality among the Corinthian believers. He wrote them a letter, which is referred to in 1 Corinthians 5:9–11 but has never been found. Some people from the household of Chloe, who may have been a member of the church in Corinth, traveled to visit Paul, and they informed him of divisive factions within the church. Before Paul could reply in writing to the church, another delegation from Corinth arrived with a letter containing questions (1 Corinthians 8:1, 16:17). Paul immediately sent Timothy to Corinth to help correct the problems (1 Corinthians 4:17), and he then wrote the letter of 1 Corinthians in anticipation that the letter would arrive even before Timothy did (1 Corinthians 16:10). The letter was likely written in 56 AD, near the end of Paul's time in Ephesus.

Paul knew from firsthand encounters that the Corinthians were proud of their knowledge and considered themselves to be spiritually mature. First Corinthians contrasts worldly and spiritual wisdom with a prevailing message that love—not knowledge—is the foundation for Christian ethics. Paul wrote to the Corinthians as their spiritual father, with fervent love but also with a strong hand of discipline. He gave specific instructions for dealing with divisions and disputes in the church, and especially for handling sexual immorality.

About the Author, the Apostle Paul. The author of this book, the apostle Paul, was in a unique position to write a theological letter to both Jewish and Gentile believers in Corinth. Paul, who received the Jewish name Saul at his birth, was born in the Roman city of Tarsus, located in Cilicia (Acts 22:3). A Hebrew by heritage, he grew up in Greek culture and obtained Roman citizenship. His family members, some of whom appear to have been wealthy and socially influential, were also citizens of Rome. Saul received the finest education available and was a strong adherent to the Law of

Moses. He became a Pharisee—the Pharisees were a leading and powerful sect in Judaism. He launched vicious attacks against the followers of Christ and was a witness to the deacon Stephen's stoning. It was while Saul was in zealous pursuit of the "followers of the Way" who had gone to Damascus, intending to persecute them even to the point of death, that he was blinded by a supernatural light and heard the voice of Jesus Christ (Acts 9:1–19). Confronted by Christ Himself, Saul's life was permanently redirected. He became as zealous a messenger for Christ as he once had been a persecutor of Christians. Changing his name to the Greek "Paul," he proclaimed Christ's "Good News" to the Gentiles with all-consuming passion, and in his lifetime, he launched at least four missionary journeys to spread the message of salvation and reconciliation with God made possible through Jesus Christ's crucifixion and resurrection. It was during his second missionary journey that he established the church in Corinth. He was assisted in his ministry there by Silas and Timothy.

AN OVERVIEW OF OUR STUDY OF THE EPISTLE OF 1 CORINTHIANS

This study guide presents seven lessons drawn from and based largely upon the Epistle of 1st Corinthians. The study guide elaborates upon, and is based upon, the commentary included in the Blackaby Study Bible:

Lesson #1: Spiritual Wisdom

Lesson #2: Sexual Purity

Lesson #3: Self-Denial

Lesson #4: The Lord's Supper

Lesson #5: Spiritual Gifts

Lesson #6: Supremacy of Love

Lesson #7: A Celestial Body

Personal or Group Use. These lessons are offered for personal study and reflection, or for small-group Bible study. The questions asked may be answered by an individual reader, or used as a foundation for group discussion. A segment titled "Notes to Leaders of Small Groups" is included at the back of this book to help those who might lead a group study of the material here.

Before you embark on this study, we encourage you to read in full the statement in the *Blackaby Study Bible* titled "How to Study the Bible." Our contention is always that the Bible is unique among all literature. It is God's definitive word for humanity. The Bible is:

- *inspired*—"God breathed"

- *authoritative*—absolutely the "final word" on any spiritual matter

- *the plumb line of truth*—the standard against which all human activity and reasoning must be evaluated

The Bible is fascinating in that it has remarkable diversity, but also remarkable unity. The books were penned by a diverse assortment of authors representing a variety of languages and cultures. The Bible as a whole has a number of literary forms. Moreover, the Bible's message from cover to cover is clear, consistent, and unified.

More than mere words on a page, the Bible is an encounter with God Himself. No book is more critical to your life. The very essence of the Bible is the Lord Himself.

God speaks by the Holy Spirit through the Bible. He also communicates during your time of prayer, in your life circumstances, and through the church. Read your Bible in an attitude of prayer, and allow the Holy Spirit to make you aware of God's activity and your personal life. Write down what you learn, meditate on it, and adjust your thoughts, attitudes, and behavior accordingly. Look for ways every day in which the truth of God's Word can be applied to your circumstances and relationships. God is not random, but orderly and intentional in the way He speaks to you.

Be encouraged—the Bible is *not* too difficult for the average person to understand if that person asks the Holy Spirit for help. (Furthermore, not even the most brilliant person can fully understand the Bible apart from the Holy Spirit's help!) God desires for you to know Him and to know His Word. Every person who reads the Bible can learn from it. The person who will receive *maximum* benefit from reading and studying the Bible, however, is the person who:

- *is born again* (John 3:3, 5). Those who are born again and have received the gift of His Spirit have a distinct advantage in understanding the deeper truths of God's Word.

- *has a heart that desires to learn God's truth.* Your attitude influences greatly the outcome of Bible study. Resist the temptation to focus on what others have said about the Bible. Allow the Holy Spirit to guide you as you study God's Word for yourself.

- *has a heart that seeks to obey God.* The Holy Spirit teaches most those who desire to apply what they learn.

Begin your Bible study with prayer, asking the Holy Spirit to guide your thoughts and to impress upon you what is on God's heart. Then make plans to adjust your life immediately to obey the Lord fully.

As you read and study the Bible, your purpose is not to *create* meaning, but to *discover* the meaning of the text with the Holy Spirit's guidance. Ask yourself, "What did the author have in mind? How was this applied by those who first heard these words?" Especially in your study of the Gospel accounts, pay attention to the words of Jesus that begin "truly, truly" or "He opened His mouth and taught them saying . . ." These are core principles and teachings that have powerful impact on *every* person's life.

At times you may find it helpful to consult other passages of the Bible (made available in the center columns in the Blackaby Study Bible), or the commentary that is in the margins of the Blackaby Study Bible.

Keep in mind always that Bible study is not primarily an exercise for acquiring information, but an opportunity for life transformation. Bible study is your opportunity to encounter God and to be changed in His presence. When God speaks to your heart, nothing remains the same. Jesus said, "He who has ears to hear, let him hear!" (Matt. 13:9). Choose to have ears that desire to hear!

The B-A-S-I-Cs of Each Study in This Guide. Each lesson in this study guide has five segments, using the word BASIC as an acronym. The word BASIC does not allude to elementary or "simple," but rather to "foundational." These studies extend the concepts that are part of the Blackaby Study Bible commentary and are focused on key aspects of what it means to be a Christ-follower in today's world. The BASIC acronym stands for:

B = *Bible Focus.* This segment presents the central passage for the lesson and a general explanation that covers the central theme or concern.

A = *Application for Today.* This segment has a story or illustration related to modern-day times, with questions that link the Bible text to today's issues, problems, and concerns.

S = *Supplementary Scriptures to Consider.* In this segment, other Bible verses related to the general theme of the lesson are explored.

I = *Introspection and Implications.* In this segment, questions are asked that lead to deeper reflection about one's personal faith journey and life experiences.

C = *Communicating the Good News.* In this segment, challenging questions are aimed at ways in which the truth of the lesson might be lived out and shared with others (either to win the lost or build up the church).

LESSON #1

SPIRITUAL WISDOM

Wisdom: the ability to use knowledge and experience to make sound and beneficial judgments and decisions

B
Bible Focus

> *We speak wisdom among those who are mature, yet not the wisdom of this age, nor of the rulers of this age, who are coming to nothing. But we speak the wisdom of God in a mystery, the hidden wisdom which God ordained before the ages for our glory, which none of the rulers of this age knew; for had they known, they would not have crucified the Lord of glory.*
>
> *But as it is written:*
>
> > *"Eye has not seen, nor ear heard,*
> > *Nor have entered into the heart of man*
> > *The things which God has prepared for those who love Him."*
>
> *But God has revealed them to us through His Spirit. For the Spirit searches all things, yes, the deep things of God. For what man knows the things of a man except the spirit of the man which is in him? Even so no one knows the things of God except the Spirit of God. Now we have received, not the spirit of the world, but the Spirit who is from God, that we might know the things that have been freely given to us by God.*
>
> *These things we also speak, not in words which man's wisdom teaches but which the Holy Spirit teaches, comparing spiritual things with spiritual. But the natural man does not receive the things of the Spirit of God, for they are foolishness to him; nor can he know them, because they are spiritually discerned. But he who is spiritual judges all things, yet he himself is rightly judged by no one. For who has known the mind of the LORD that he may instruction Him? But we have the mind of Christ (1 Corinthians 2:6–16).*

Not all wisdom is equal. The apostle Paul made it very clear to the Corinthians that spiritual wisdom differs from the wisdom of the natural man. The spiritual wisdom is revealed through Christ Jesus, and the key to understanding God's wisdom is rooted in our relationship with the Spirit. Only God can know God, and therefore no individual has the ability to know God or God's wisdom apart from the Holy Spirit. The Greeks had a philosophy that "like is known only by like." Paul builds upon this understanding to explain godly wisdom.

Natural or human wisdom occurs when a person "studies"—gaining information, which progresses to understanding of how information combines to create concepts and principles, which progresses to wisdom of how and when certain concepts and principles might be effectively applied to life situations. To gain earthly wisdom, one must be a student of life and the natural world, including human behavior.

Spiritual wisdom develops along a different path—a person is presented the Gospel of Jesus Christ, including an understanding of His character and His acts of redemption, and the Holy Spirit then imparts an understanding that reveals what Jesus would do and say in any given circumstance or situation in the life of a believer. To gain spiritual wisdom, one must have a saving knowledge of Jesus Christ, and be led by the Holy Spirit on a daily basis. To gain spiritual wisdom, one must be in relationship with God.

In the passage above, Paul states that natural man considers the things of God to be "foolishness." This word in the Greek means dull, tasteless, insipid—in other words, of little interest and undesirable. For the believer, however, God's wisdom includes the capacity to discern all things associated with truth, excellence, and beauty. Spiritual wisdom is to be highly prized. Spiritual wisdom is the key to seeing the world as Jesus saw the world, and responding to it as Jesus did.

Throughout this letter to the Corinthians, the apostle Paul paints a vivid portrait of the person who is spiritually wise. Such a person:

- glories in the Lord (1:31)

- is meek and humble (2:3)

- relies on the power of God (4:20)

- is submitted to spiritual leadership (14:37, 16:16)

- acknowledges God as the source of everything (6:19–20)

- serves others and seeks the well-being of others (8:1, 10:20)

- stands up under temptation (10:13)

- maintains self-control and discipline (6:12, 9:27)

- has enduring power (3:10–14)

In sharp contrast, the person who functions according to "worldly wisdom" is a person who boasts in men (3:21), is arrogant or "puffed up" (4:6), relies on self and the power of words (4:20), criticizes leadership (4:8), takes pride in personal accomplishments (4:7), insists on personal rights and is insensitive to others—often wounding others (8:9,11–12), is subject to "falling" into temptation and sin (10:12), and often does not endure in the faith (3:15).

Whom do you consider in your world today to be spiritually wise?

How does this person live?

What are that person's foremost character traits?

What are the benefits of spiritual wisdom in that person's life?

Now take a look in your own spiritual mirror. In what ways do you sense a need for greater spiritual wisdom?

How will you go about acquiring it?

A
Application for Today

Several years ago, a major revival broke out in an area of West Africa after the first ten chapters of Leviticus were read aloud in the Lobi language to an audience in Burkina Faso. This audience of subsistence farmers, poison-arrow warriors, and animistic mask-makers was fascinated by what they heard. The public reading of Leviticus, which was followed up by a presentation of the Gospel, was the catalyst for many conversions to Christ Jesus.

"Leviticus?" you may be saying. It is not a book that most Christians would consider to be pertinent to evangelism. Indeed, many Christians are likely to admit that they have never read the entire Book of Leviticus!

The vast majority of western Christians seem quick to identify themselves as "New Testament" believers. They often don't see God's wisdom in the Old Testament.

We must never forget that Jesus knew the Old Testament Scriptures extremely well. Young men in His day memorized the first five books of the Old Testament (Genesis, Exodus, Leviticus, Numbers, and Deuteronomy) by the time they were 12 years old. Many of Jesus' statements were associated with phrases or verses from the Old Testament.

The Holy Spirit challenges us to apply the WHOLE of God's Word—both the written Word of God and the life of Jesus the Word—to the WHOLE of our lives. To know how to apply God's Word, and truly to be spiritually wise, we must first know the concepts and principles that Jesus knew.

A second factor to consider is this: We live in an "information age" that has resulted in increased specialization. More facts are readily available to the average person than ever before, and certainly more information is available than might be learned by any one person. Specialization is one of the results of this information overload. In nearly every career field we see a growing number of specialties with each passing decade. The phrase "Renaissance person"—a person who is well-versed in a wide variety of subjects from science to the arts to literature—is becoming less and less known in our world today.

We don't go to a doctor—we go to a cardiologist, pediatrician, or dermatologist.

We don't go to a lawyer—we go to a patent attorney, personal liability attorney, or an estate attorney.

We don't get a liberal arts and sciences degree—we "major" in biology and minor in Spanish.

What is *your* career field or area of study?

What specialties are associated with that field?

Many of us also don't read the whole of God's Word—we read the Gospels and our favorite epistles and psalms.

How does this concept of increased specialization affect the church? Is there a fragmenting of our understanding of Scripture? Is there an overemphasis on certain aspects of Christian living, or on a specific gift of the Spirit?

S
Supplementary Scriptures to Consider

Spiritual wisdom is not only the foundation on which the church is to be built, but it is the heart of spiritual unity. The church in Corinth had become contentious— some claiming that they were of Paul's group, others that they were of Apollos' group, and still others claiming, "I am of Cephas" or "I am of Christ." The apostle Paul wrote with heartfelt urgency:

> I plead with you, brethren, by the name of our Lord Jesus
> Christ, that you all speak the same thing, and that there be
> no divisions among you, but that you be perfectly joined
> together in the same mind and in the same judgment
> (1 Corinthians 1:10–11).

• Spiritual wisdom is the wisdom of God—it is cohesive, unified, and "one" in its message. At times, however, some in the church claim that they have the wisdom of God, yet are in disagreement with others. What must be done in those instances?

• How can people of different backgrounds be "perfectly joined" and have the "same mind" and "same judgment" in the church?

The opposite of spiritual wisdom, for the apostle Paul, was the carnal mind, which led to envy, strife, and divisions:

> I, brethren, could not speak to you as to spiritual people but as to carnal, as to babes in Christ. I fed you with milk and not with solid food; for until now you were not able to receive it, and even now you are still not able; for you are still carnal. For where there are envy, strife, and divisions among you, are you not carnal and behaving like mere men? For when one says, "I am of Paul," and another, "I am of Apollos," are you not carnal? Who then is Paul, and who is Apollos, but ministers through whom you believed, as the Lord gave to each one? I planted, Apollos watered, but God gave the increase. So then neither he who plants is anything, nor he who waters, but God who gives the increase. Now he who plants and he who waters are one, and each one will receive his own reward according to his own labor. For we are God's fellow workers; you are God's field, you are God's building" (1 Corinthians 3:1–9).

• The wisdom of God is a collective wisdom—no one person has the FULL wisdom of God, but every person who seeks spiritual wisdom is granted specific insight into the wisdom of God. Why is it important that we focus on the Lord and share our insights into His nature and His word?

• How do you define the word "cooperate"?

• How do unity and diversity work together?

The results of spiritual wisdom is seen in the demonstration of the power of God:

> My speech and my preaching were not with persuasive words of human wisdom, but in demonstration of the Spirit and of power, that your faith should not be in the wisdom of men but in the power of God" (1 Corinthians 2:5).

- Do you believe it is possible for a person to have genuine spiritual power apart from spiritual wisdom?

- Why is it necessary to have spiritual wisdom in the exercise of spiritual power?

I
Introspection and Implications

1. The educational world measures IQ—intelligence quotient—and the psychiatric world now has measures for EQ—emotional quotient. What do you believe would be the factors for discerning SWQ—spiritual wisdom quotient?

2. What do you believe is the role of spiritual wisdom in exercising all gifts given by the Holy Spirit?

3. What do you believe is the relationship between godly character and spiritual wisdom?

4. Why do you believe spiritual wisdom is important to acquire? How does it relate to the practicalities of your personal work, ministry, and relationships?

C
Communicating the Good News

What is the importance of spiritual wisdom to evangelism? Why must we seek and acquire godly wisdom as we seek to share the Gospel with an individual or group?

LESSON #2

SEXUAL PURITY

Fornication: sexual intercourse between two consenting adults who are not married to each other
Adultery: voluntary sexual relations between a married person and somebody other than his or her spouse

B
Bible Focus

> Do you not know that your bodies are members of Christ? Shall I then take the members of Christ and make them members of a harlot? Certainly not! Or do you not know that he who is joined to a harlot is one body with her? For the two," He says, "shall become one flesh." But he who is joined to the Lord is one spirit with Him.
>
> Flee sexual immorality. Every sin that a man does is outside the body, but he who commits sexual immorality sins against his own body. Or do you not know that your body is the temple of the Holy Spirit who is in you, whom you have from God, and you are not your own? For you were bought at a price; therefore glorify God in your body and in your spirit, which are God's (1 Corinthians 6:15–20).
>
> It is actually reported that there is sexual immorality among you, and such sexual immorality as is not even named among the Gentiles—that a man has his father's wife! And you are puffed up, and have not rather mourned, that he who has done this deed might be taken away from among you. For I indeed, as absent in body but present in spirit, have already judged (as though I were present) him who has so done this deed. In the name of our Lord Jesus Christ, when you are gathered together, along with my spirit, with the power of our Lord Jesus Christ, deliver such a one to Satan for the destruction of the flesh, that his spirit may be saved in the day of the Lord Jesus.
>
> Your glorying is not good. Do you not know that a little leaven leavens the whole lump? Therefore purge out the old leaven, that you may be a new lump, since you truly are unleavened. For indeed Christ, our Passover, was sacrificed for us. Therefore let us keep the feast, not with old leaven, nor with the leaven of malice and wickedness, but with the unleavened bread of sincerity and truth (1 Corinthians 5:1–8).

The apostle Paul was appalled that a member of the church would have "his father's wife." This woman, of course, was not the man's mother, and in all likelihood, the father had died, but the net result was that a man had entered into a sexual relationship with his stepmother. While most of us Christians today would be equally appalled at this, we must recognize that the world as a whole would *not* be scandalized. This is the normal fodder for many a day-time television soap-opera plot! Neither would the general population of Corinth have been scandalized. This was normal sexual behavior for that city, although Paul directly indicates that the "moral" people in the secular world at large would have found this specific relationship undesirable.

We need to recognize that the norms of sexual behavior of the world at large differ greatly from the norms presented in God's Word. The Bible calls for Christians to refrain from acts of sexual impurity and sexual indiscretions in all their many forms. We are to cultivate and practice sexual purity and fidelity in our pursuit of emotional and spiritual faithfulness. As Christians we are not to have a sexual relationship apart from a spouse within the parameters of a marriage vow. That means no fornication, no adultery, no dalliances, no infidelity, and no "affairs of the heart."

The Corinthian church had to contend with the worship of the goddess Aphrodite, goddess of love. Within the temple grounds, pagans worshipped Aphrodite by engaging in sexual behavior with designated temple prostitutes, both men and women. This is an especially important fact to consider as we read Paul's words, "Do you not know that your body is the temple of the Holy Spirit who is in you?"

Our deepest and most intimate relationship is to be with the Lord. Any relationship that we have with another person must be one that submits to and honors the central covenant we have with Christ Jesus.

Paul raises a second concern: The Corinthian believers appear to have been very quick to take offense at any suggestions that this sinful relationship needed to be purged from their midst. It isn't a matter of being quick to forgive and restore. It is a matter that this man and his wife have refused to repent and seek forgiveness. The Corinthian church had allowed their relationship to continue without change, adopting something of an "ongoing forgiveness" policy that does not require any behavioral change on the part of those involved in the illicit relationship.

Do bodies of believers continue to do the same in today's world? Without doubt.

Christian behavior and attitudes are *not* to be those of the world at large.

Change from "old worldly ways" to "new godly ways" is to be the norm. We are to grow up in Christ as we mature spiritually, which means that we become more and more like Christ Jesus in thought, word, deed, and character. We are to embody less and less of the character, behavior, and attitudinal norms of the world around us.

Are your ideas about sexual behavior and sexual purity different since you accepted Christ Jesus as your Savior and Lord? If not, why?

The second issue is one that also commands our attention: At what point do you insist that others in the church refrain from sexual impropriety? At what point do you set standards of behavior that are required for full participation in the life of the church? Is it at the point of appointing leadership? Extending church membership? Baptizing? Conducting a marriage ceremony?

What should be the approach to those who are engaging in sinful sexual activity and may not even know that what they are doing is sin?

A
Application for Today

A number of years ago, a professor in a secular university hosted a Bible study in her home for her former students. She was not a religion teacher, per se, but she was a Christian. And, a number of her students had expressed an interest in learning more about the Christian faith. One night during their study they came across a passage related to sexual impurity. A discussion ensued. This professor said later, "I was shocked. The students thought impurity related to taking a bath before and after having sex! Some had read the word 'unclean' about sexual impurity. It never dawned on them that sexual behavior was to be reserved for marriage."

This professor decided to do a specific study of the Scriptures on sexual behavior and the Bible study became focused on this topic for several weeks. She made more surprising discoveries as her former students read and discussed various Bible passages. She learned: her students did not know what the word "fornication" meant, they saw nothing wrong with oral sex between unmarried people, and they had never been taught that sexual intercourse prior to marriage or between unmarried people was wrong (although they believed adultery was wrong and that married people should be faithful to their spouses). Repeatedly, the students referred to the images and sexual innuendos of movies, television programs, magazines, and popular books as being their primary sources of information about sex and proper sexual behavior. The students, as a whole, were stunned to discover that "casual sex" was totally prohibited by God's Word. They were surprised that their professor believed it was immoral to have a child out of wedlock.

When the teacher asked several students privately what they had learned at church or in Sunday school about appropriate sexual behavior for Christians, they each told her, "Nothing. The topic of sex was never brought up."

Evaluate your own opinions about sexual behavior.

Consider what your children—or grandchildren, or the children in your church youth group—may know, or don't know, about godly sexual behavior.

What needs to be said that isn't being said? By whom?

S
Supplementary Scriptures to Consider

Paul knew that it was impossible for the Corinthian believers to abstain totally from all contact with immoral people. If they had adopted that isolationist tactic, they would have had far less opportunity to witness for Christ. Rather, Paul wrote:

> I wrote to you in my epistle not to keep company with sexually immoral people. Yet I certainly did not mean with the sexually immoral people of this world, or with the covetous, or extortioners, or idolaters, since then you would need to go out of the world. But now I have written to you not to keep company with anyone named a brother, who is sexually immoral, or covetous, or an idolater, or a reviler, or a drunkard, or an extortioner— not even to eat with such a person. For what I have I to do with judging those also who are outside? Do you not judge those who are inside? But those who are outside God judges. Therefore "put away from yourselves the evil person' " (1 Corinthians 5:9–13).

• In what way are the standards of the church to be obviously higher— more moral—than the standards of the world?

• To what extent are we as Christians to have "contact" with those who are unbelievers?

• What boundaries do we need to place on our relationships with Christians who continue to engage in immoral or unethical behavior?

Paul wrote very specifically about the moral boundaries related to sexual behavior and marriage:

> It is good for a man not to touch a woman. Nevertheless, because of sexual immorality, let each man have his own wife, and let each woman have her own husband. Let the husband render to his wife the affection due her, and likewise also the wife to her husband. The wife does not have authority over her own body, but the husband does. And likewise the husband does not have authority over his own body, but the wife does. Do not deprive one another except with consent for time, that you may give yourselves to fasting and prayer; and come together again so that Satan does not tempt you because of your lack of self-control. But I say this as a concession, not as a commandment. For I wish that all men were even as I myself. But each one has his own gift from God, one in this manner and another in that. But I say to the unmarried and to the widows: It is good for them if they remain even as I am; but if they cannot exercise self-control, let them marry. For it is better to marry than to burn with passion (1 Corinthians 7:1–9).

• Paul was not opposed to celibacy as a way of life, but he was opposed to unilateral celibacy within a marriage and he did recognize that not all single people can maintain a successful celibate life. What sexual pressures do you see placed today on those who are single? What stigma, if any, do you see attached to celibacy?

• How difficult is it to remain sexually pure in today's culture?

• In what ways do you regard celibacy as a "gift from God"?

Paul recognized that in times of crisis or persecution, marriage places added stress on a person's life. He wrote this to the Corinthians:

> Now concerning virgins: I have no commandment from the Lord; yet I give judgment as one whom the Lord in His mercy has made trustworthy. I suppose therefore that this is good because of the present distress—that it is good for a man to remain as he is. Are you bound to a wife? Do not seek to be loosed. Are you loosed from a wife? Do not seek a wife. But even if you do marry, you have not sinned; and if a virgin marries, she has not sinned. Nevertheless such will have trouble in the flesh, but I would spare you (1 Corinthians 7:25–29).

- What do you believe Paul meant when he said that those who marry have "trouble in the flesh"? Why do most people in our society today believe that single people have more "trouble" sexually than married people?

- Many people in our world today believe that the "ideal state"—or "normal state"—is for a person is to be married and have a family. Paul seems to argue that remaining single and becoming married are equally acceptable, even normal, in God's eyes. What is your conclusion regarding the advantages or disadvantages of being single versus being married?

Purity extends to all of life, not only to one's sexual behavior.

> Do not be unequally yoked together with unbelievers. For what fellowship has righteousness with lawlessness? And what communion has light with darkness? And what accord has Christ with Belial? Or what part has a believer with an unbeliever? And what agreement has the temple of God with idols? For you are the temple of the living God. As God has said:
>
> "I will dwell in them
>   And walk among them.
>   I will be their God,
>   And they shall be My people."
>   (Leviticus 26:12, Jeremiah 32:38, Ezekiel 37:27)
> Therefore

"Come out from among them
  And be separate, says the Lord.
  Do not touch what is unclean,
  And I will receive you." (Isaiah 52:11, Ezekiel 20:34,41)
"I will be a Father to you,
  And you shall be My sons and daughters,
  Says the LORD Almighty."
  (2 Samuel 7:14, 2 Corinthians 6:14–18)

- To what degree and in what ways does God's Word call us to be "separated" from the world?

- In what ways do you find it personally difficult to be "in the world" but not "of the world"?

I
Introspection and Implications

1. What challenges regarding sexual purity have you faced personally? How did you deal with those challenges?

2. How do you teach your children about sexual purity when it seems that so many television programs, movies, and popular songs have a sexual innuendo or explicit sexual images associated with them?

3. Why do you believe God calls His people to be pure and "separate" from an impure world?

4. What stance do you believe the church should take regarding those in the church who are sexually impure but remain unrepentant, even to the point of being unconcerned about their behavior?

C
Communicating the Good News

As counterintuitive as it may seem, many unbelievers who live sexually impure lives find purity a very appealing concept. How might a message of "purity" be incorporated into a presentation of the Gospel? How might purity and evangelism blend?

LESSON #3

SELF-DENIAL

Stumbling block: anything that stands in the way of achieving a goal or understanding of something

B
Bible Focus

> Now concerning things offered to idols: We know that we
> all have knowledge. Knowledge puffs up, but love edifies. And
> if anyone thinks that he knows anything, he knows nothing yet
> as he ought to know. But if anyone loves God, this one is
> known by Him.
>
> Therefore concerning the eating of things offered to idols,
> we know that an idol is nothing in the world, and that there is
> no other God but one. For even if there are so-called gods,
> whether in heaven or on earth (as there are many gods and
> many lords), yet for us there is one God, the Father, of whom
> are all things, and we for Him; and one Lord Jesus Christ,
> through whom are all things, and through whom we live.
>
> However, there is not in everyone that knowledge; for some,
> with consciousness of the idol, until now eat it as a thing
> offered to an idol; and their conscience, being weak, is defiled.
> But food does not commend us to God; for neither if we eat
> are we the better, nor if we do not eat are we the worse.
>
> But beware lest somehow this liberty of yours become a
> stumbling block to those who are weak. For if anyone see you
> who have knowledge eating is an idol's temple, will not the
> conscience of him who is weak be emboldened to eat those
> things offered to idols? And because of your knowledge shall
> the weak brother perish, for whom Christ died? But when you
> thus sin against the brethren, and wound their weak con-
> science, you sin against Christ. Therefore, if food makes my
> brother, stumble, I will never again eat meat, lest I make my
> brother stumble (1 Corinthians 8:1–13).

Is it better to be right or to be loving? The apostle Paul clearly comes
down on the side of *loving* in his letter to the Corinthians.

What is the issue involved? In the pagan Greek temples, animals were
routinely sacrificed to false gods. The meat from those animals was then sold
in special "temple markets." The Greeks who worshiped the pantheon of
Greek gods believed that to eat meat offered to an idol—which was repre-
sentative of the god—was a form of "identification" with the god. The
consumption of the meat was therefore an act of pagan worship, intended to

convey a message to the god and to others, "I am sitting at the same table as this god and we share the same substance." The questions arose for the church in Greek cities with such temples and shrines: Should a Christian shop at such a market? Should a Christian serve meat purchased at such a market?

Some in the Corinthian church argued that, since idols and false gods weren't "real"—they had no power and had no divine nature—there should be no limits on the purchase or consumption of this meat. Good meat was good meat! They contended to those who opposed the purchase and consumption of such meats, "Get your thinking straight. This meat isn't tainted in any way and you should grow up spiritually and get over any concern you have."

Others claimed that the practice of shopping in these markets and serving meat that had been offered to false gods sent the wrong signal to unbelievers or people who were new to the Christian faith. They did not believe that Christians should identify *in any way* with pagan worship practices. They contended, "Christians should know better than to participate in even the least Greek temple practice."

The apostle Paul said, "It isn't a matter of whether you 'know better' or 'know what's right.' The issue is whether you are operating in LOVE toward others. Love and not knowledge is the basic ground rule for Christian conduct. LOVE is what counts!"

Knowledge can be dangerous when it is not governed by God's love. As Christians, we are wise to seek to prove our love, not our knowledge. In the end, we are accountable to God not for how much we knew in our lifetime, but for how well we have loved those whom the Lord has placed in our lives.

The question that we face today is probably not related to "meat" at all, but it certainly may be related to whether alcohol is purchased or served at a meal, whether tobacco products are offered at the end of a meal, or to various other practices related to things that we eat, drink, wear, or do.

What sorts of behaviors might cause a Christian brother or sister to "stumble" in their walk with the Lord? What is our responsibility to ensure that we do nothing that might cause another believer to falter or fail in his or her Christian walk?

How difficult is it to give up something that we find pleasurable and acceptable for the purpose of helping another person grow in his or her faith?

A
Application

For years, women wore hats to church in the United States. In many places around the world, women *still* wear hats or some form of head covering to worship services, believing very strongly that it is a sign of reverence for a woman to cover her head in the presence of the Lord. The practice is regarded as a sign of humility and respect.

The apostle Paul addressed this issue in writing to the Corinthians, but without a direct argument related to love. He wrote:

> "Every man praying or prophesying, having his head
> covered, dishonors his head. But every woman who prays or
> prophesies with her head uncovered dishonors her head,
> for that is one and the same as if her head were shaved."
> (1 Corinthians 11:4–5)

Are we in error today by *not* encouraging women to wear hats or head coverings to church?

What about the woman who has never worn a hat to church and suddenly finds herself in a situation where a hat is "expected"? What should an American tourist do, for example, when visiting a Christian church in another nation where head covering for women is the norm? Is it wrong for an American female tourist to go to a church service without a hat? Is it wrong for the host church to look down on a female tourist who arrives with an uncovered head?

Ah but what about the homeless person who shows up unshaven, unkempt, and perhaps with inappropriate shoes or shirt at a church service in the United States?

What should be said and done?

S
Supplementary Scriptures to Consider

The apostle Paul also wrote other messages on this theme to the Corinthians:

> All things are lawful for me, but not all things are helpful:
> all things are lawful for me, but not all things edify. Let no
> one seek his own, but each one the other's well-being
> (1 Corinthians 10:23).

- How do you determine what is in the general interest of another person's well-being?

> Whether you eat or drink, or whatever you do, do all to the
> glory of God. Give no offense, either to the Jews or to the
> Greeks or to the church of God, just as I also please all men in
> all things, not seeking my own profit, but the profit of many,
> that they may be saved (1 Corinthians 10:31–33).

- How do you define, in terms of practical behaviors, the word "edify" (build up, strengthen) when it comes to one or more specific relationships in your life?

- How do you determine if another person is feeling offended by what you do?

• If you discover that you have offended another person, what should you do?

The prophet Isaiah spoke about the Messiah as someone who would "not break a bruised reed"—a concept very close to the apostle Paul's admonition that a person should not cause a weaker brother or sister in Christ to stumble:

> Behold! My Servant whom I uphold,
> My Elect One in whom My soul delights!
> I have put My Spirit upon Him;
> He will bring forth justice to the Gentiles.
> He will not cry out, nor raise His voice,
> Nor cause His voice to be heard in the street.
> A bruised reed He will not break,
> And smoking flax He will not quench;
> He will bring forth justice for truth.
> He will not fail nor be discouraged,
> Till He has established justice in the earth;
> And the coastlands shall wait for His law."
> (Isaiah 42:1–4: see also Matthew 12:18–21)

• What does it mean to refrain from breaking a bruised reed?

• How did Jesus embody this passage?

• What is the message to us as we attempt to win others to Christ?

I
Introspection and Implications

1. Have you ever been made to feel "stupid"—facing expectations that you should have known something that you didn't know? How did you feel? What did you do? How do you feel today as you remember that time? What are the feelings you had then—and now—for the person who made you stupid?

2. Have you ever felt embarrassed because you felt that you were inappropriately dressed for a particular occasion? Who made you feel embarrassment? The host? The other guests? Did you feel embarrassed even though nobody else at the event considered you inappropriately addressed—in other words, were you embarrassed for no reason?

3. To what extent do we each strive to live up to the expectations of other people? To what extent *should* we yield to the expectations of others?

4. In what ways is it important to honor and show respect to the beliefs of others? In what situations should we speak up for what we know to be true? Is it loving tolerance or cowardice to remain silent when you know that someone is making a serious error that could have eternal consequences?

5. Think back to the way in which you first "learned Christ." Did you come to know Christ Jesus as your personal Savior because of someone who loved you, or because of someone who taught you? Was there a balance between loving and teaching? How might you describe such a balance?

6. There's a saying, "People don't know what they don't know." How can you discover what you don't know . . . that you should know or need to know? How can you encourage another person to discover what he doesn't know . . . that you believe he should know or needs to know?

C
Communicating the Good News

There's a popular saying today: "Nobody cares what you know until they know that you care." How did this apply to the Church? How does it apply to your personal witness for Christ Jesus?

To what degree do we allow very young children to make "social mistakes," regarding these errors as areas for future training? In like manner, to what degree should we allow new believers to make "tradition mistakes?"

Are errors connected to tradition different than errors connected to theology?

How should we determine when to step in and teach or train, and when to stay silent?

LESSON #4

THE LORD'S SUPPER

Communion: a feeling of emotional or spiritual closeness, often based upon shared religious identity and beliefs, fellowship Holy Communion: a sacrament of consecrated bread and wine taken in commemoration of Jesus Christ

B
Bible Focus

> When you come together as a church, I hear that there are
> divisions among you, and in part I believe it. For there must
> also be factions among you, that those who are approved may
> be recognized among you. Therefore when you come together
> in one place, it is not to eat the Lord's Supper. For in eating,
> each one takes his own supper ahead of others; and one is
> hungry and another is drunk. What! Do you not have houses
> to eat and drink in? Or do you despise the church of God and
> shame those who have nothing? What shall I say to you? Shall
> I praise you in this? I do not praise you.
>
> For I received from the Lord that which I also delivered to
> you: That the Lord Jesus on the same night in which He was
> betrayed took bread; and when He had given thanks, He broke
> it and said, "Take, eat; this is My body which is broken for
> you; do this in remembrance of Me." In the same manner He
> also took the cup after supper, saying, "This cup is the new
> covenant in My blood. This do, as often as you drink it, in
> remembrance of Me.,"
>
> For as often as you eat this bread and drink this cup, you
> proclaim the Lord's death till He comes.
>
> Therefore whoever eats this bread or drinks this cup of the
> lord in an unworthy manner will be guilty of the body and
> blood of the Lord. But let a man examine himself, and so let
> him eat of the bread and drink of the cup. For he who eats and
> drinks in an unworthy manner eats and drinks judgment to
> himself, not discerning the Lord's body. For this reason many
> are weak and sick among you, and many sleep. For if we
> would judge ourselves, we would not be judged. But when we
> are judged, we are chastened by the Lord that we may not be
> condemned with the world.
>
> Therefore, my brethren, when you come together to eat,
> wait for one another. But if anyone is hungry, let him
> eat at home, lest you come together for judgment
> (*1 Corinthians 11:18–34*).

The **Bible** tells us that, after Jesus ascended to heaven, the Holy Spirit had
been poured out on the day of Pentecost, and the church had been formed,
the new believers in Christ Jesus met daily in one public area of the Temple
grounds to share their faith as well as their material substance. This was not

just a nicety—for many it was a necessity. The new believers in Jerusalem frequently were ostracized from their families and their places of employment, solely because they had accepted Jesus as their Savior. Meeting with other believers gave these estranged Jews-turned-Christian the courage to remain steadfast in their faith, gave them the fellowship of a new "family," and on a very practical level, gave them the food, shelter, and material support to stay alive and care for their children. We read in the Acts of the Apostles: "They continued steadfastly in the apostles' doctrine and fellowship, in the breaking of bread, and in prayers" (Acts 2:12).

In the earliest days of the church, the meal shared by the believers was a complete meal, probably what we would call today a "potluck" supper. The suppers were daily, so any person in need within the new church might have the assurance that he or she would have sufficient food for each day.

The meals themselves were book-ended with bread and wine. A Jewish meal began with bread, similar to pita bread today. This practice of serving bread at the beginning of a meal continues today in most restaurants! In Jesus' day, a piece of bread was used as a utensil to scoop up or sop up food from other dishes—such as salads, yogurt, stews, and soups—that were placed on low tables to be enjoyed "family style." Bread was regarded as the staple of life. Even if no other food was served, bread could sustain life.

A typical Jewish meal ended with a small glass of wine, intended as a taste of sweetness and for digestive purposes. Wine was regarded also as a symbol of joy and satisfaction. The phrase "bread and wine," therefore, came to be synonymous among the believers with a FULL meal that was both satisfying and nourishing—physically, emotionally, and spiritually.

Unfortunately, some of those coming to these communal meals were arriving early and eating and drinking too much. Those who arrived late found little or nothing left for them. Paul says to the church in Corinth: Pay attention to what you are doing when you engage in any communal meal! Do what Jesus would do—treat others as you would desire to be treated if you were in their shoes. Be intentional about how you eat and drink, including how much you are eating and drinking, and why!"

Paul then makes a similar plea to the way in which a person takes the elements of Communion—bread and wine. Be intentional! Don't just partake of these elements in a ritualized manner without being fully aware of what you are doing and why. Nothing about eating the Lord's Supper should ever be done in a thoughtless, careless, or routine manner. The Lord's Supper *must* be a time for serious reflection and of total identification with Christ Jesus. The elements of bread and wine are ones that JESUS said would be His body and His blood to us. These elements link us to Him and to one another in a way that is a profound and desirable spiritual mystery.

The terms, *Lord's Supper, Communion, Holy Communion, Eucharist, The Lord's Table*, all refer to the act of commemorating Christ's sacrificial death on the cross. The church uses bread and wine (many use juice) during a time of worship.

How does or should a shared potluck at church differ from any other mealtime in a person's life?

How does partaking of the Lord's Supper differ from a church potluck? These are questions worthy of deep consideration.

What does taking the bread and wine of the Lord's Supper mean to *you*?

What difference does it make in *your* life to partake of Christ's body and blood in a Communion service?

A
Application for Today

Not long ago, a woman wrote a letter to the national publication of her church denomination that she was "very proud" that her church had opened its communion table to people of all beliefs. Buddhists, Hindus, Muslims, atheists, and people of all other religious faiths were being invited to attend services at her church, which called itself a Christian body of believers. All of those attending were openly invited to partake of the bread and wine of the Lord's Supper as a means of "building community" and "fostering peace."

Another member of this denomination responded in the next edition of the publication, "Communion is not a variation of a wine and cheese party. It is not a form of 'refreshments' to enjoy after a lecture!"

What do you think the apostle Paul would have said to this particular church? How had they changed the meaning of the Lord's Supper from what Christ intended? Do you think that people who deny the Lordship of Christ should participate in an activity designed to commemorate His sacrifice?

What would you say to a person who saw the practice of a come-one-come-all Communion table as a sign of being spiritually enlightened and community minded in relation to what you know of the culture in Corinth?

S
Supplementary Scriptures to Consider

The apostle Paul shared with the Corinthians what Jesus had revealed to him about the Last Supper. For an eyewitness account of the Last Supper we must turn to the Gospels:

And as they were eating, Jesus took bread, blessed and broke it, and gave it to the disciples and said, "Take, eat; this is My body."

Then He took the cup, and gave thanks, and gave it to them, saying, "Drink from it, all of you. For this is My blood of the new covenant, which is shed for many for the remission of sins. But I say to you, I will not drink of this fruit of the vine from now on until that day when I drink it new with you in My Father's kingdom" (Matthew 26:26–29).

• What does partaking of Holy Communion mean to you?

• How does participating with others in a Communion service create a sense of "family" among believers in the church?

• How does participating in a Communion service help you to identify more fully with the life and death of Jesus Christ?

This is how the Gospel of Luke presents the Last Supper:

> When the hour had come, He sat down, and the twelve apostles with Him. Then He said to them, "With fervent desire I have desired to eat this Passover with you before I suffer, for I say to you, I will no longer eat of it until it is fulfilled in the kingdom of God."
>
> Then He took the cup, and gave thanks, and said, "Take this and divide it among yourselves, for I say to you, I will not drink of the fruit of the vine until the kingdom of God comes."
>
> And He took bread, gave thanks and broke it, and gave it to them, saying, "This is My body which is given for you; do this in remembrance of Me."
>
> Likewise He also took the cup after supper, saying, "This cup is the new covenant in My blood, which is shed for you."

• In what ways is Jesus our "spiritual staple"—the giver and sustainer of our spiritual life?

• The Jews believed strongly that "life is in the blood"—the flow of blood was a strong sign to them that a person was alive. In what ways does Jesus give us spiritual life?

I
Introspection and Implications

1. What does it mean to you to have communion (or fellowship) with another person?

2. What does it mean to you to have communion (or fellowship) with God?

3. What does it mean to you to share Holy Communion with other believers?

C
Communicating the Good News

Communion services are often puzzling to new believers, as well as to unbelievers who attend a church service in which the Lord's Supper is administered or a Eucharist service is celebrated. How would you explain Holy Communion to a person who might be puzzled at what he or she encounters in *your* church?

How would you explain to an unbeliever that the Lord's Supper or Holy Communion is for "believers only"—what reasons would you give?

LESSON #5
SPIRITUAL GIFTS

Gift: something presented to person meant for his benefit or use in service to others

B
Bible Focus

> *Now concerning spiritual gifts, brethren, I do not want you
> to be ignorant: You know that you were Gentiles, carried away
> to these dumb idols, however you were led. Therefore I make
> known to you that no one speaking by the Spirit of God calls
> Jesus accursed, and no one can say that Jesus is Lord except
> by the Holy Spirit.*
>
> *There are diversities of gifts, but the same Spirit. There are
> differences of ministries, but the same Lord. And there are
> diversities of activities, but it is the same God who works all
> in all. But the manifestation of the spirit is given to each one
> for the profit of all: for to one is given the word of wisdom
> through the Spirit, to another the word of knowledge through
> the same Spirit, to another faith by the same Spirit, to another
> gifts of healings by the same Spirit, to another the working of
> miracles, to another prophecy, to another discerning of spirits,
> to another different kinds of tongues, to another the interpreta-
> tion of tongues. But one and the same Spirit works all these
> things, distributing to each one individually as He wills.*
>
> *For as the body is one and has many members, but all
> members of that one body, being many, are one body, so also
> is Christ. For by one Spirit we were all baptized into one
> body—whether Jews or Greeks, whether slaves or free—and
> have all been made to drink into one Spirit. For in fact the
> body is not one member but many . . . .*
>
> *Now you are the body of Christ, and members individually.
> And God has appointed these in the church: first apostles,
> second prophets, third teachers, after that miracles, then gifts
> of healings, helps, administrations, varieties of tongues. Are
> all apostles? Are all prophets? Are all teachers? Are all
> workers of miracles? Do all have gifts of healings? Do all
> speak with tongues? Do all interpret? But earnestly desire the
> best gifts (1 Corinthians 12:1–12, 27–31).*

The issues that Paul raises in this passage go far beyond an inventory of
spiritual gifts at work in the Corinthian church. They are issues that we face
today, regardless of our denomination or our beliefs about manifestations of
the Holy Spirit. On the one hand are the concepts of individualism, diversity,
and uniqueness. On the other hand are the concepts of community, unity, and
commonality. At what point should our individuality shine and be devel-

oped? At what point must our individuality yield to a greater concern for the whole?

From the beginning, the church has had diversity of form, rituals, and procedures. At the same time, the church has been called to tremendous unanimity of belief and values. Perhaps nowhere in the entire New Testament is a more powerful statement made than this one by Paul: "There are diversities of gifts, but the same Spirit. There are differences of ministries, but the same Lord. And there are diversities of activities, but it is the same God who works all in all."

The church is like a massive and brilliantly polished diamond with many facets, each of which serves to refract the intense and magnificent Light of the whole.

Paul's purpose is not a comprehensive listing of the gifts imparted by the Holy Spirit, nor a definition of them. His purpose is a statement that all things in the church must be subjected to and governed by the Holy Spirit. Very specifically:

- all gifts, ministries, and activities in the church should convey this message to the unbeliever and believer alike, "Jesus is Lord."

- all genuine spiritual gifts are resident in the Holy Spirit and cannot be grasped or attained apart from the Holy Spirit.

- the Holy Spirit imparts various manifestations of His own character and identity to various individuals, but always with the intent of bringing benefit to the whole of the church.

These, then, become the three foremost criteria, by which all ministries, activities, and spiritual gifts should be evaluated in any church body:

- Is Jesus lifted up as Savior and Lord?

- Are people engaging in ministries, activities, and exercise of spiritual gifts on their own strength and for their own self-advancement, or are they engaging in ministries, activities, and the practice of spiritual gifts to build up others and lead others into a fuller and deeper relationship with God?

- Does the ministry, activity, or manifestation of the gift benefit everybody in the church?

Not everybody in any church functions in the same gifts, is involved in the same ministries, or participates in the same activities. All, however, can evaluate their own involvement in the church by asking of themselves about each class they take, ministry they start, committee they join, and gift of their talent and service, "Am I doing this to lift up the Lord Jesus? Am I trusting the Lord to lead and help me, or am I trying to do this on my own? Am I seeking the good of everyone else in the church?"

The Holy Spirit delights in meeting ALL of the spiritual needs of the church, and He alone is capable of fully defining those needs, orchestrating the solutions to all problems, and using every person in the church at some level and in some way to accomplish HIS purposes. The Holy Spirit is the One who knits us together as a genuine body, functioning as a living organism and not as just another organization. He is the One who imparts unity and reconciliation to highly diverse and distinctively different individuals. He is the Giver of Life to every cell in the Body of Christ.

A
Application for Today

A solo part in a children's pageant many years ago gave a little girl a life-changing opportunity to sing these profound words to those in attendance: "I'm just a little toe, and I'm here so you will know God's love."

Every person, no matter how young or seemingly insignificant, is part of the Body of Christ and has a purpose, role, and opportunity to express God's love. This includes children as well.

Too often, however, we tend to ask of the children's program in our churches: "Are the children having a good time at church?" or, "Are the children learning God's Word?" or, "Are the children learning the songs and rituals of the church so they will fit in fully as they grow up?" The real questions that we perhaps should be asking are these:

- Are the children coming to acceptance of Jesus as their Savior?

- Are the children learning how to praise and exalt Jesus as their Lord?

- Are the children being encouraged to invite other children to church?

- Are the children being taught how to pray for themselves and other people?

- Are the children being taught how to tell their friends about Jesus?

- Are the children being taught how to rely upon the Holy Spirit to help them every day—at school, at home, and at play?

- Are the children ALREADY being incorporated into the full life of the church? Do they feel as if they are an integral and important part of the entire Body?

The Holy Spirit desires to use children in ways that are profound and deeply meaningful. We must never relegate children or teenagers to second-tier involvement in the church, or think that as they accept Jesus as their personal Savior and seek to follow Him as their Lord, they receive or function in only a "pint-sized" portion of the Holy Spirit.

Can you think of a time where a child challenged you in your faith?

How do the children in *your* church use their gifts to glorify God?

S
Supplementary Scriptures to Consider

Paul used the metaphor of the human body to explain diversity of gifts and purposes in the church:

> If the foot should say, "Because I am not hand, I am not of the body," is it therefore not of the body? And if the ear should say, "Because I am not an eye, I am not of the body," is it therefore not of the body? And if the ear should say, "Because I am not an eye, I am not of the body," is it therefore not of the body? If the whole body were an eye, where would be the hearing? If the whole were hearing, where would be the smelling? But now God has set the members, each one of them, in the body just as He pleased. And if they were all one member, where would be the body? (1 Corinthians 12:15–19)

- Why is diversity important for the healthy functioning of a church?

> But now indeed there are many members, yet one body. And the eye cannot say to the hand, I have no need of you"; nor again the head to the feet, "I have no need of you." No, much rather, those members of the body which seem to be weaker

are necessary. And those members of the body which we think to be less honorable, on these we bestow greater honor; and our unpresentable parts have greater modesty, but our presentable parts have no need. But God composed the body, having given greater honor to that part which lacks it, that there should be no schism in the body, but that the members should have the same care for one another. And if one member suffers, all the members suffer with it; or if one member is honored, all the members rejoice with it (1 Corinthians 12:20–26).

• It is clear from Paul's metaphor that we *need* one another in the Body of Christ.

• Do you have a sense that you need other believers in your church? Why or why not?

• Why do we sometimes seem jealous of the gifts or role another person plays in the church? Why do we tend to regard some positions as more desirable than others?

- Thinking specifically of your church, do you see evidence that "if one member suffers, all the members suffer with it; or if one member is honored, all the members rejoice with it?" Why or why not?

Paul regarded "prophecy"—the forthtelling or proclaiming of God's Word—to be the pinnacle of spiritual gifts:

> Pursue love, and desire spiritual gifts, but especially that you may prophesy (1 Corinthians 14:1).

- Why is prophecy (or preaching the fullness of the Bible) vital to the spiritual health of a church?

- In what ways might an individual "prophesy"—proclaim the truth of God's Word—to himself?

In addition to spiritual gifts, Paul saw a diversity of expression as being valuable to a healthy church:

> How is it then, brethren? Whenever you come together, each of you has a psalm, has a teaching, . . . has a revelation. Let all things be done for edification (1 Corinthians 14:26).

• How can you determine if a message, teaching, or song has "edification" value to all who are present in a church service?

• Note that Paul admonishes the Corinthian believers that "each" of them come to church services prepared to share something of a spiritual nature with the others who are present. In what ways might this be done today in a large church?

Paul was supremely concerned that church services be conducted in an orderly manner:

> For God is not the author of confusion but of peace, as in all the churches of the saints (1 Corinthians 14:33).

- What are the advantages of a church service in which all things are conducted in an orderly manner?

- How is "confusion" counterproductive to learning, understanding, or gaining spiritual wisdom? How is "confusion" counterproductive to genuine spiritual growth?

I
Introspection and Implications

1. If you were to do an inventory of the spiritual gifts, ministries, and activities in your church, what would you list under each of the headings below?
   SPIRITUAL GIFTS
   MINISTRIES
   ACTIVITIES

2. Does diversity of gifts, ministries, and activities in your church produce strength and cohesion, or fragmentation and chaos? Why do you believe this to be so?

Do these various gifts, ministries, and activities blend together in a cohesive manner, or do they seem to function independently and without focused leadership?

3. Have you identified your own personal spiritual gifts, ministries, and activities that the Lord is prompting you to develop and pursue? Are you becoming *increasingly more involved* in the life of your church and in the lives of fellow believers? Why or why not?

4. Do you struggle in your relationship with others who have spiritual gifts or ministries that differ from your gifts and ministries? How might this struggle be resolved?

C
Communicating the Good News

In what ways do all spiritual gifts, ministries, and activities find common ground in evangelism?

Why is it important that our evangelistic outreach efforts have a diversity of spiritual gifts?

In what ways might it be possible to have an "evangelistic outreach" embedded in every small group, Sunday school class, or activity of the church?

Lesson #6

SUPREMACY OF LOVE

Love: an act of the will that expresses tender affection or compassion

B
Bible Focus

> Though I speak with the tongues of men and of angels, but
> have not love, I have become sounding brass or a clanging
> cymbal. And though I have the gift of prophecy, and under-
> stand all mysteries and all knowledge, and though I have all
> faith, so that I could remove mountains, but have not love, I
> am nothing. And though I bestow all my goods to feed the
> poor, and though I give my body to be burned, but have not
> love, it profits me nothing.
>
> Love suffers long and is kind; love does not envy; love does
> not parade itself, is not puffed up; does not behave rudely,
> does not seek its own, is not provoked, thinks no evil; does not
> rejoice in iniquity, but rejoices in the truth; bears all things,
> believes all things, hopes all things, endures all things.
>
> Love never fails. But whether there are prophecies, they will
> fail; whether there are tongues, they will cease; whether there
> is knowledge, it will vanish away. For we know in part and we
> prophesy in part. But when that which is perfect has come,
> then that which is in part will be done away.
>
> When I was a child, I spoke as a child, I understood as a
> child, I thought as a child; but when I became a man, I put
> away childish things. For now we see in a mirror, dimly, but
> then face to face. Now I know in part, but then I shall know
> just as I also am known.
>
> And now abide faith, hope, love, these three; but the
> greatest of these is love (1 Corinthians 13:1–13).

The apostle Paul clearly stated to the Corinthians that far more important
than any spiritual gift, ministry, or activity, is the presence of God's love
freely flowing in our individual lives and in the church as a whole. We must
never lose sight of the fact that the twelfth chapter of 1 Corinthians on
spiritual gifts leads to the thirteenth chapter of 1 Corinthians on the supremacy of love.

At the end of this magnificent chapter, which some have called one of the
foremost literary statements in all of history, Paul notes that the Holy Spirit
imparts three gifts that are in contrast to those that the Holy Spirit distributes
"to each one individually as He wills" (1 Corinthians 12:11). These three
great gifts are called "abiding"—they last, they remain, they are constants in
the life of every genuine believer.

The Holy Spirit is the One who imparts a measure of FAITH to each of us. It is faith that enables us to accept Jesus as our Savior and follow Him daily as our Lord.

The Holy Spirit is the One who imparts HOPE to our hearts, especially the hope of heaven and the fullness of its glory. It is hope that comforts us at all times and gives us the compelling courage to take risks of faith, and to believe for the fulfillment of all God's promises in our lives.

The Holy Spirit is also the One who imparts to us the greatest of the "abiding gifts"—LOVE. It is love that enables us to build sound, lasting, and precious relationships in the Body of Christ. It is love that binds us together in unity, regardless of the diversity of our gifts, talents, personalities, and backgrounds.

Those things which we do without the love of the Holy Spirit are of little consequence. Those things which we do WITH the love of the Holy Spirit flowing in us and through us are of profound effect.

Stop to reflect for a moment about what genuine love from another person means to you. What happens in *you* when you experience love that manifests itself in the forms described below?

• Someone has great patience with you, far beyond anything you "deserve"

• Someone is very kind to you, far beyond anything you "warrant"

• Someone deals with you without any envy or pride

• Someone extends great courtesy to you, giving you a preferred position or allowing you to "go first" or "be first"

• Someone is generous toward you, but without any intent of manipulation and without seeking to receive anything back from you

• Someone voices that he or she is believing the best for you and that they also see the best in you

• Someone comes quickly to your defense when you are falsely accused or attacked

• Someone rejoices with you when things go well for you

• Someone puts up with your bad moods, faults, and failures, and continues to believe that all things will work to your eventual and eternal good

• Someone hopes with you for God's best at all times

• Someone refuses to leave you and seeks instead to "stick with you" in an hour of need

This type of love is invaluable! It is what causes us to grow and mature in Christ Jesus. This type of love builds us up on the inside so that we truly feel cherished, not only by the person extending such love, but cherished by God Himself.

This type of love is not something that we can manufacture on our own. It is not an ideal that we can achieve by trying. It is love that is possible only as we allow the Holy Spirit to flow through us to others.

Ask God today to impart to you His abiding gifts in greater and greater quantity.

A
Application for Today

The city of Corinth was famous in the first century for producing some of the finest bronze mirrors in antiquity. No matter how polished the bronze, however, to look into a bronze mirror was to have only partial reflection. The apostle Paul used the analogy of looking in a mirror and seeing "dimly" as a metaphor for describing the way that we perceive our own lives, the lives of others, and the greater mysteries of God. The truth of this is profound in the light of Paul's message about love:

- We love ourselves, and thus others *as ourselves*, only to the extent that we see ourselves as Christ see us.

- We love others in most cases only to the extent that we truly "see others" as Christ sees them.

How do you believe Christ Jesus sees you?

How do you believe He loves you?

Are you willing to admit that Christ Jesus "sees you" far more accurately than you see yourself, and that He loves you far more than you love yourself?

What kind of courage does it take to ask God to help you see others as He sees them? In what ways are we then compelled to love others and to give to them?

S
Supplementary Scriptures to Consider

The Gospels and New Testament books agree—loving God and loving others go hand in hand. The Epistle of First John tells us:

> "If someone says, 'I love God,' and hates his brother, he is a liar; for he who does not love his brother whom he has seen, how can he love God whom he has not seen? And this commandment we have from Him: That he who loves God must love his brother also" (1 John 4:20–21).

• Why is loving a Christian brother or sister an essential part of loving God?

• How does a person determine the most loving thing to do for another person?

Jesus said this about the love that He wanted His followers to have for one another:

> As the Father loved Me, I also have loved you; abide in My love. If you keep My commandments, you will abide in My love, just as I have kept My Father's commandments and abide in His love.

These things I have spoken to you, that My joy may remain in you, and that your joy may be full. This is My command-ments, that you love one another as I have loved you. Greater love has no one than this, than to lay down one's life for his friends. You are My friends if you do whatever I command you . . . . These things I command you, that you love one another" (John 15:9–14,17).

• In what ways do you believe our love for one another brings joy into our lives?

• How do you respond to the fact that Jesus *commanded* us as His followers to love one another?

• What does it mean to you to love others *as* Christ loves you?

• Apart from sacrificial martyrdom, how do we lay down our lives for others?

Love is not a New Testament concept alone. It is at the heart of the Old Testament law:

> You shall not hate your brother in your heart. You shall surely rebuke your neighbor, and not bear sin because of him. You shall not take vengeance, nor bear any grudge against the children of your people, but you shall love your neighbor as yourself: I am the LORD (Leviticus 19:17–18).

• How do you respond to these verses from the Old Testament?

Jesus clearly identified the two great commandments at the heart of all other commandments in the Bible:

> Jesus said to him, "You shall love the LORD your God with all your heart, with all our soul, and with all your mind." This is the first and great commandment. And the second is like it: "You shall love your neighbor as yourself." On these two commandments hang all the Law and the Prophets." (Matthew 22:37–40)

- What does it mean to you to love God with all your heart? With all your soul? With all your mind?

- Is the *way* that we love God similar to the way that we love ourselves? Is the *way* that we love God similar to the way that we are to love others? If not, what are the differences?

I
Introspection and Implications

1. How do you define "God's love" (agape love)? In what ways is it different from human, brotherly love?

2. Whom do you consider to be a worthy recipient of your love? Why?

3. Is there any person from whom you would withhold your love? Why?

4. Do you ever struggle in loving yourself according to the criteria in 1 Corinthians 13?

C
Communicating the Good News

Why must all evangelistic efforts be steeped in God's love?

How might we best portray God's love to a person who is filled with anger or hatred?

In what ways are we who believe in Jesus Christ as our Savior and Lord challenged in our presentation of the Gospel to people in false religions who hate Christianity?

LESSON #7

A CELESTIAL BODY

Celestial: belonging to, suitable for, or typical of heaven Terrestrial: relating to Earth and living on land

B
Bible Focus

> *But someone will say, "How are the dead raised up? And with what body do they come?" Foolish one, what you sow is not made alive unless it dies. And what you sow, you do not sow that body that shall be, but mere grain—perhaps wheat or some other grain. But God gives it a body as He pleases, and to each seed its own body.*
>
> *All flesh is not the same flesh, but there is one kind of flesh of men, another flesh of animals, another of fish, and another of birds.*
>
> *There are also celestial bodies and terrestrial bodies, but the glory of the celestial is one, and the glory of the terrestrial is another. There is one glory of the sun, another glory of the moon, and another glory of the stars; for one star differs from another star in glory.*
>
> *So also is the resurrection of the dead. The body is sown to corruption, it is raised in incorruption. It is sown in dishonor, it is raised in glory. It is sown in weakness, it is raised in power. It is sown a natural body, it is raised a spiritual body. There is a natural body, and there is a spiritual body. And so it is written, "The first man Adam became a living being." The last Adam became a life-giving spirit.*
>
> *However, the spiritual is not first, but the natural, and afterward the spiritual. The first man was of the earth, made of dust; the second Man is the Lord from heaven. As was the man of dust, so also are those who are made of dust; and as is the heavenly Man, so also are those who are heavenly. And as we have borne the image of the man of dust, even shall we also bear the image of the heavenly Man* (1 Corinthians 15:35–49).

One prominent theme in ancient Greek philosophy contended that everything spiritual is intrinsically good and everything physical is intrinsically evil. To those who had held this view prior to coming to Christ, the idea of a resurrected body would have been repugnant, if not unthinkable. Paul presented what was essentially a "new idea" to the Corinthians: the physical and spiritual are related—they are not poles apart, but rather, they are connected in a mysterious but observable way. Just as a seed is planted into the ground and "dies" as it begins to grow to into a plant, so our physical bodies die and are buried and we are transformed into a new likeness. A seed of corn is called "corn" and a stalk of corn is called "corn" and in a similar manner, we remain the same and yet are different. The seed and plant look nothing alike, and yet are mysteriously linked as one—the "fullness of the plant" resides fully in the seed. Our present and future bodies are similarly linked.

Paul also noted for the Corinthians that our resurrection is like that of Jesus. We are given a new body for a new heavenly home.

The Gospel accounts tell us this about Jesus' resurrected body:

- He could pass through shut doors (John 20:19 26)

- His disciples could touch him (Luke 24:39, John 20:17, 27)

- He could vanish quickly from view (Luke 24:31)

- He was able to eat (Luke 24:42–43)

- He could speak and be heard (John 21 and Acts 1:1–8)

- His disciples recognized Him (John 21:1–7. Mark 16:12–14)

Paul was quick to assure the Corinthians that their new spiritual bodies after death would be incorruptible, honorable, glorious, and strong.

What a future awaits those who die in Christ! Truly death is only a transformation moment that begins a process of eternal life and growth.

What are *your* hopes for *your* eternal future?

A
Application for Today

"Will I recognize you in heaven?" a little boy asked his Grandpa.

"Sure," Grandpa replied.

"But how?" the little boy asked.

"Do you remember seeing the picture of your mother on our refrigerator door? That picture was taken 20 years ago and your mother looks very different today. But when your Mom asked you whose picture it was, you didn't even hesitate for a second in saying back to her, 'It's YOU, Mom.'"

"I remember," the little boy said.

"How did you know that the person in the picture was your mother when the person in the picture doesn't look just like your Mom looks today?" Grandpa asked.

The little boy thought for a moment and then said, "I knew it was Mom because nobody else has that look in her eyes."

Philosophers and poets alike have noted for millennia that the eyes are the windows into the soul of a person. What resides within us—our eternal spirit made alive in Christ by the power of the Holy Spirit—does not die. It is the "real" us.

What do you learn about a person by looking deeply into this or her eyes?

Why do we often divert our gaze or desire *not* to maintain long eye contact with another person?

If you knew that a person was only going to be able to see the BEST of you by looking into your eyes, would you be more willing to maintain long eye contact with that person?

S
Supplementary Scriptures to Consider

Two of the greatest hopes in Christianity are the hope of resurrection and the hope of heaven. What an awesome thing to have a resurrected body alive forever in an eternal home!

> Now I saw a new heaven and a new earth, for the first heaven and the first earth had passed away. Also there was no more sea. Then I, John, saw the holy city, New Jerusalem, coming down out of heaven from God, prepared as a bride adorned for her husband. And I heard a loud voice from heaven saying, "Behold, the tabernacle of God is with men, and He will dwell with them, and they shall be His people. God Himself will be with them and be their God. And God will wipe away every tear from their eyes; there shall be no more death, nor sorrow, nor crying. There shall be no more pain, for the former things have passed away" (Revelations 21:1–4).

• What are your hopes for your life after death?

• What do you believe heaven will be like *for you*?

• What are you looking most forward to doing or experiencing in heaven?

I
Introspection and Implications

1. In an age when superheroes are common fare in television programs and movies —and in an age when "special effects" make the supernatural seem real—fewer and fewer people seem to talk about the *realities* of a heavenly home and a resurrected body. Stop to reflect about your own hopes regarding your eternal future.

2. The Bible does not tell us in detail about our life in heaven. Why do you think heaven and the ongoing splendors of eternity have been kept as one of God's mysteries?

3. Is the human heart and mind ever capable of encompassing the concepts of "infinity," "eternity," or "unending life"?

C
Communicating the Good News

Jesus said that those who believe in Him and receive Him as their Savior will receive forgiveness of sins and life everlasting. This message must be central to all evangelistic outreaches. Eternal life and eternal death are both presented in the Bible. Man is given the option of choice. When was the last time you had an opportunity to present the Gospel to someone who had not accepted Jesus as God's chosen Son? What did you say about the eternal consequences associated with making, or not making, a decision to receive Jesus as Savior?

Though heaven is a future reward, eternal life with God is achieved at the moment that we place our faith in Christ. How can aspects of heaven be experienced here on earth?

NOTES TO LEADERS
OF SMALL GROUPS

As the leader of a small discussion group, think of yourself as a facilitator with three main roles:

- Get the discussion started

- Involve every person in the group

- Encourage an open, candid discussion that remains Bible focused

Be aware that group members may have a wide range of knowledge of the Bible. Some may not know where to find the book that you are studying, while others can tell you the outline from memory. You certainly don't need to be the person with all the answers! In truth, much of your role is to be a person who asks questions:

- What really impacted you most in this lesson?

- Was there a particular part of the lesson, or a question, that you found troubling?

- Was there a particular part of the lesson that you found encouraging or insightful?

- Was there a particular part of the lesson that you'd like to explore further?

Express to the group at the outset of your study that your goal as a group is to gain new insights into God's Word—this is not the forum for defending a point of doctrine or a theological opinion. Stay focused on what God's

Word says and means. The purpose of the study is also to share insights on how to apply God's Word to everyday life. *Every* person in the group can and should contribute—the collective wisdom that flows from Bible-focused discussion is often very rich and deep.

Seek to create an environment in which every member of the group feels free to ask questions of other members in order to gain greater understanding. Encourage the group members to voice their appreciation to one another for new insights gained, and to be supportive of one another personally. Take the lead in doing this. Genuinely appreciate and value the contributions made by each person.

You may want to begin each study by having one or more members of the group read through the section provided under "Bible Focus." Ask the group specifically if it desires to discuss any of the questions under the "Application" section . . . the "Supplemental Scriptures" section . . . and the "Implications" and "Communicating the Gospel" section. You do not need to bring closure—or come to a definitive conclusion or consensus—about any one question asked in this study. Rather, encourage your group that if the group does not *have* a satisfactory Bible-based answer to a question that the group engage in further "asking . . . seeking . . . and knocking" strategies to discover the answers! Remember the words of Jesus: "Ask, and it will be given to you, seek, and you will find; knock, and it will be opened to you. For everyone who asks receives, and he who seeks finds, and to him who knocks it will be opened" (Matthew 7:7–8).

Finally, open and close your study with prayer. Ask the Holy Spirit, whom Jesus called the Spirit of Truth, to guide your discussion and to reveal what is of eternal benefit to you individually and as a group. As you close your study, ask the Holy Spirit to seal to your remembrance what you have read and studied, and to show you ways in the upcoming days, weeks, and months *how* to apply what you have studied to your daily life and relationships.

General Themes for the Lessons

Each lesson in this study has one or more core themes. Continually pull the group back to these themes. You can do this by asking simple questions, such as, "How does that related to _____ ?" "How does that help us better understand the concept of _____ ?" "In what ways does that help us apply the principle of _____ ?"

A summary of general themes or concepts in each lesson is provided below:

Lesson #1
SPIRITUAL WISDOM

Spiritual wisdom vs. natural wisdom

Characteristics of the spiritually wise person

Developing the mind of Christ

Unity and diversity in the Body of Christ

The role of spiritual wisdom in the church

Lesson #2
SEXUAL PURITY

The challenge of remaining sexually pure in a sex-crazed society

Celibacy

Purity

The challenges of being single in a mostly-married world

The challenges of being married in a world that seems to have a singles-have-more-fun attitude

Lesson #3
SELF-DENIAL

Stumbling blocks

Being offended, offending others

Edification

Lesson #4
THE LORD'S SUPPER

Holy Communion vs. communion

The Body of Christ

The Blood of Christ

Lesson #5
SPIRITUAL GIFTS

Diversity of gifts, same Spirit

Diversity of ministries, same Lord

Diversity of activities, same God

Lesson #6

SUPREMACY OF LOVE

The three abiding gifts—faith, hope, and love

The attributes of godly love

Godly love vs. brotherly love

The challenge of loving the unlovable

The challenge of loving those who are filled with anger, hatred, or prejudice against us

Lesson #7

A CELESTIAL BODY

Resurrected body

Heavenly home

Everlasting life

NOTES

NOTES

NOTES

NOTES

NOTES

NOTES

NOTES

NOTES